Wrap-n-Bake
Egg Rolls

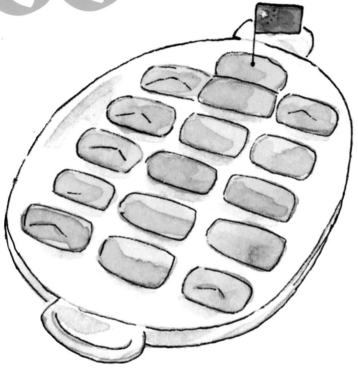

and Other Chinese Dishes

by Nick Fauchald   Illustrated by Ronnie Rooney

Special thanks to our content adviser:
Joanne L. Slavin, Ph.D., R.D.
Professor of Food Science and Nutrition
University of Minnesota

Picture Window Books
Minneapolis, Minnesota

Editor: Shelly Lyons   Designer: Tracy Davies
Page Production: Melissa Kes

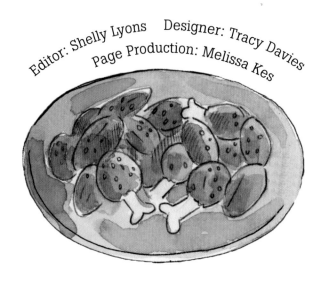

Art Director: Nathan Gassman   Editorial Director: Nick Healy
Creative Director: Joe Ewest
The illustrations in this book were created with watercolor and pen and ink.

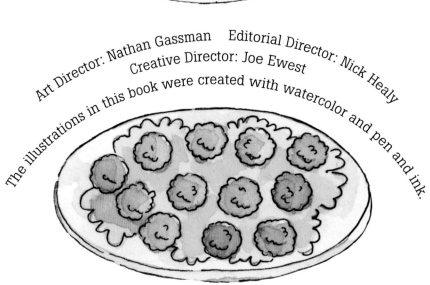

Picture Window Books • 151 Good Counsel Drive • P.O. Box 669 • Mankato, MN 56002-0669
877-845-8392 • www.picturewindowbooks.com

The illustration on page 4 is from *www.mypyramid.gov.*

Printed in the United States of America.

 All books published by Picture Window Books are manufactured
with paper containing at least 10 percent post-consumer waste.

Library of Congress Cataloging-in-Publication Data
Fauchald, Nick.
Wrap-n-bake egg rolls : and other Chinese dishes / by Nick Fauchald ; illustrated by Ronnie Rooney.
p. cm. — (Kids dish)
Includes bibliographical references and index.
ISBN 978-1-4048-5183-2 (library binding)
1. Cookery, Chinese—Juvenile literature. I. Rooney, Ronnie. II. Title.
TX724.5.C5F397 2009
641.5951—dc22   2009002753

Editor's note: The author based the difficulty levels of the recipes on the skills and time required, as well as the number of ingredients and tools needed. Adult help and supervision is required for all recipes.

Table of Contents

EASY

INTERMEDIATE

ADVANCED

MyPyramid

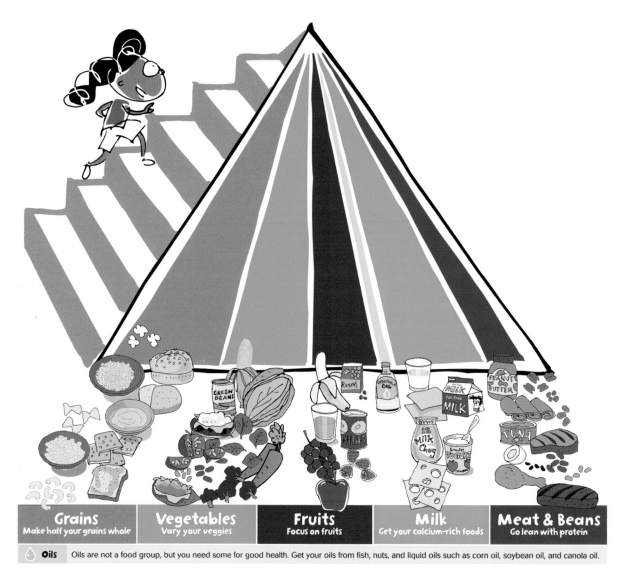

Grains	Vegetables	Fruits	Milk	Meat & Beans
Make half your grains whole	Vary your veggies	Focus on fruits	Get your calcium-rich foods	Go lean with protein

◯ **Oils** Oils are not a food group, but you need some for good health. Get your oils from fish, nuts, and liquid oils such as corn oil, soybean oil, and canola oil.

In 2005, the U.S. government created MyPyramid, a plan for healthy eating and living. The new MyPyramid plan contains 12 separate diet plans based on your age, gender, and activity level. For more information about MyPyramid, visit *www.mypyramid.gov*.

The pyramid at the top of each recipe shows the main food groups included. Use the index to find recipes that include food from the food group of your choice, major ingredients used, recipe levels, and appliances/equipment needed.

New York–based **Nick Fauchald** is the author of numerous children's books. He helped create the magazine *Every Day with Rachael Ray* and has been an editor at *Food & Wine* and *Wine Spectator* magazines. Nick attended the French Culinary Institute in Manhattan and has worked with some of the world's best chefs. However, he still thinks kids are the most fun to cook with.

Dear Kids,

China is one of the world's oldest civilizations, dating back thousands of years. And many of your favorite Chinese dishes, such as fried rice and dumplings, have been around for almost as long. This book contains simplified versions of these and other recipes, which are easy enough for you to cook with only a little help from an adult. Along the way, you'll learn about Chinese culture and how the country's most famous foods have also become some of America's favorites. Happy cooking!

Cooking is fun, and safety in the kitchen is very important. As you begin your cooking adventure, please remember these tips:

★ Make sure an adult is in the kitchen with you.
★ Tie back your hair and tuck in all loose clothing.
★ Read the recipe from start to finish before you begin.
★ Wash your hands before you start and whenever they get messy.
★ Wash all fresh fruits and vegetables.
★ Take your time cutting the ingredients.
★ Use oven mitts whenever you are working with hot foods or equipment.
★ Stay in the kitchen the entire time you are cooking.
★ Clean up when you are finished.

Now, choose a recipe that sounds tasty, check with an adult, and get cooking. Your friends and family are hungry!

Enjoy,
Nick

Note to Adults:

Learning to cook is an exciting, challenging adventure for young people. It helps kids build confidence; learn responsibility; become familiar with food and nutrition; practice math, science, and motor skills; and follow directions. Here are some ways you can help kids get the most out of their cooking experiences:

• Encourage them to read the entire recipe before they begin cooking. Make sure they have everything they need and understand all of the steps.

• Make sure young cooks have a kid-friendly workspace. If your kitchen counter is too high for them, offer them a step stool or a table to work at.

• Expect new cooks to make a little mess, and encourage them to clean it up when they are finished.

• Help multiple cooks divide the tasks before they begin.

• Enjoy what the kids just cooked together.

Special Tips and Glossary

beating eggs: Using a whisk or fork, stir the eggs quickly until they have a froth.

cracking eggs: Tap the egg on the counter until it cracks. Hold the egg over a small bowl. Gently pull the two halves of the shell apart until the egg falls into the bowl.

measuring dry ingredients: Measure dry ingredients (such as flour and sugar) by spooning the ingredient into a measuring cup until the cup is full. Then level off the top of the cup with the back of a table knife.

measuring wet ingredients: Place a clear measuring cup on a flat surface, then pour the liquid into the cup until it reaches the correct measuring line. Be sure to check the liquid at eye level.

bake: cook food in an oven

blend: mix together completely

chop: cut food into small pieces of similar size

cool: set hot food on a wire rack until it's no longer hot

cover: put a container lid, plastic wrap, or aluminum foil over a food; use aluminum foil if you're baking the food, and plastic wrap if you're chilling, freezing, microwaving, or leaving the food on the counter

drain: pour off a liquid, leaving the food behind; usually done with a strainer or colander

grate: reduce a food, such as cheese, to small particles by rubbing on a grater

ladle: use a ladle to spoon a liquid into a bowl

line: cover the inside of

preheat: turn an oven on before you use it; it usually takes about 15 minutes to preheat an oven

simmer: keep food on the stove just below or at the boiling point

spread: make an even layer of something soft, such as mayonnaise or frosting

sprinkle: scatter something in small bits

stir: mix ingredients with a spoon until blended

strain: pour off a liquid, leaving the food behind; usually done with a strainer or colander

toss: mix ingredients together with your hands or two spoons until blended

whisk: stir a mixture rapidly until it's smooth

METRIC CONVERSION CHART

1/4 teaspoon (1.25 milliliters)
1 teaspoon (5 milliliters)
2 teaspoons (10 milliliters)

1 tablespoon (15 milliliters)
2 tablespoons (30 milliliters)
3 tablespoons (45 milliliters)

1/4 cup (60 milliliters)
1/3 cup (80 milliliters)
1/2 cup (120 milliliters)

3/4 cup (180 milliliters)
1 cup (240 milliliters)
1 1/2 cups (360 milliliters)
2 cups (480 milliliters)
4 cups (960 milliliters)
5 cups (1,200 milliliters)

8 ounces (224 grams)
10 ounces (280 grams)
16 ounces (448 grams)

1 pound (450 grams)
2 pounds (900 grams)

TEMPERATURE CONVERSION CHART

375° Fahrenheit (191° Celsius)
400° Fahrenheit (204° Celsius)
425° Fahrenheit (218° Celsius)
475° Fahrenheit (246° Celsius)

Kitchen Tools

HERE ARE THE TOOLS YOU'LL USE WHEN COOKING THE RECIPES IN THIS BOOK★

3-inch-round cookie cutter or drinking glass

8-by-8-inch baking dish

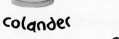
aluminum foil

blender

colander

cooking spray

cutting board

fork

garlic press

grater

kitchen shears

ladle

large pot

clear measuring cup

measuring cups

measuring spoons

microwave-safe bowls

mixing bowls

nontoxic marker or pen

oven mitts

paper towels

pastry brush

plastic wrap

rimmed baking sheets

platter

rolling pin

serrated knife

large saucepan

slips of paper

small, sharp knife

serving bowls

soup bowls

spoon

metal steaming basket

strainer

table knife

metal tongs

whisk

wooden spoons

VEGETABLES, MEAT & BEANS

This healthy side dish is flavored with Chinese five-spice powder, a mixture of cinnamon, cassia buds, star anise, ginger, and cloves.

Five-Spice Broccoli

INGREDIENTS
one 2-inch piece of peeled
  fresh ginger
one 10-ounce bag frozen
  broccoli spears
2 tablespoons unsalted
  butter
2 teaspoons soy sauce
1/4 teaspoon Chinese
  five-spice powder
1/3 cup chopped roasted
  peanuts

TOOLS
grater
paper towels
measuring spoons
drinking glass
saucepan
oven mitts
medium-sized
  mixing bowl
small microwave-safe
  bowl
wooden spoons

1 Grate the ginger onto a paper towel. Squeeze the grated ginger into a drinking glass, until you have 1 teaspoon of juice. Throw away the remaining ginger.

2 Ask an adult to cook the broccoli in a saucepan until crisp-tender. Place the cooked broccoli in a medium-sized mixing bowl.

3 Meanwhile, place the butter, ginger juice, soy sauce, and five-spice powder in a small microwave-safe bowl. Heat the mixture in the microwave until the butter is melted, about 45 seconds.

4 Toss the broccoli with the melted butter mixture. Sprinkle with the peanuts, and serve.

In China, it's a tradition to eat noodles on your birthday. The long noodles symbolize a long, happy life.

Birthday Noodles

1 In a blender, combine the peanut butter with the water, soy sauce, sesame oil, and honey. Blend until smooth.

2 Ask an adult to cook the noodles according to package directions. Drain the cooked noodles in a colander.

3 In a medium-sized mixing bowl, toss the noodles and the peanut butter sauce until coated. Refrigerate until cold.

4 With a kitchen shears, cut the scallion greens crosswise into 1/4-inch pieces.

5 Serve the cold noodles with the scallion greens, peanuts, and bean sprouts.

INGREDIENTS

3 tablespoons smooth peanut butter
1/4 cup hot water
2 tablespoons soy sauce
1 tablespoon sesame oil
2 teaspoons honey
8 ounces spaghetti noodles
2 scallions
3/4 cup chopped roasted peanuts
1 cup bean sprouts, optional

TOOLS

blender
measuring spoons
clear measuring cup
large pot
oven mitts
colander
medium-sized mixing bowl
wooden spoons
kitchen shears
measuring cups

This chewy dessert is called *babao fan* in China. It is named after eight kinds of fruits and nuts traditionally added to the sweet, sticky rice.

Eight Treasures Pudding

INGREDIENTS

4 cups warm sticky rice (also called sweet rice)

1/3 cup honey

2 cups assorted chopped dried fruit, such as raisins, cherries, cranberries, dates, or apricots

1/2 cup assorted chopped nuts, such as peanuts, almonds, or walnuts

TOOLS

mixing bowls
fork
measuring cups
spoon
cooking spray
wooden spoon
plastic wrap
platter

Have an adult prepare the sticky rice according to package instructions. In a large mixing bowl, use a fork to mix the warm rice with the honey.

In a small mixing bowl, mix the dried fruit with the nuts.

Spray the inside of a medium-sized bowl with cooking spray. Spread a handful of the fruit and nuts in the bottom of the bowl.

Cover the fruit and nuts with a thin layer of the rice. Add another layer of fruit and nuts, then another layer of rice. Repeat until you've used up all the remaining ingredients (the top layer should be rice).

FOOD FACT★ Eight Treasures pudding is traditionally served on the seventh day of the first month of the Chinese lunar calendar. This day marks the end of the Chinese New Year.

5 Cover the bowl with plastic wrap, and press down firmly on the rice. Refrigerate for 2 hours.

6 Remove the plastic wrap, and tip the bowl of rice pudding upside-down onto a platter.

7 Serve.

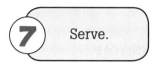

VEGETABLES
This Recipe Includes

This dish is named after a province in southwestern China, where the food is known for its bold, spicy flavors.

Sichuan Bold Beans

INGREDIENTS

3 garlic cloves, peeled
one 1-inch piece of fresh, peeled ginger
1 scallion
2 teaspoons vegetable oil
2 teaspoons soy sauce
2 teaspoons rice vinegar
8 ounces green beans, trimmed

TOOLS

grater
8-by-8-inch microwave-safe baking dish
kitchen shears
measuring spoons
wooden spoon
oven mitts

1 Finely grate the garlic cloves and ginger into the baking dish.

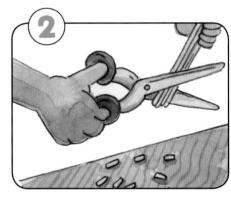

2 With a kitchen shears, cut the scallion greens into pieces. Add to the garlic and ginger.

3 Add the oil, and stir to coat.

4 Ask an adult to microwave the mixture, uncovered, for 2 minutes. Remove the dish from the microwave.

NUTRITION NOTE★ Green beans are full of vitamin K and fiber. Vitamin K is important for maintaining healthy blood. Fiber is good for digestion.

Add the remaining ingredients, and toss to coat.

Ask an adult to cook the beans, uncovered, until crisp-tender, about 10 minutes. Stir a few times while cooking. Remove the dish from the microwave.

 Stir the beans. Serve them hot or cold.

GRAINS, VEGETABLES,
MEAT & BEANS

In China, many dishes are served alongside lettuce leaves, which are used as wraps.

Hoisin Chicken Lettuce Wraps

INGREDIENTS

1/3 cup hoisin sauce
2 teaspoons Asian
   chili-garlic sauce
1 tablespoon rice vinegar
2 tablespoons soy sauce
2 cups shredded
   cooked chicken
8 large butterhead or iceberg
   lettuce leaves
1/2 cup crispy rice noodles
   or chow mein noodles

TOOLS

medium-sized
   microwave-safe bowl
clear measuring cup
measuring spoons
measuring cups
wooden spoons
plastic wrap
oven mitts
spoon
platter

14

In a medium-sized microwave-safe bowl, stir the hoisin sauce with the chili sauce, rice vinegar, and soy sauce.

Add the chicken, and toss to coat.

Cover the bowl with plastic wrap. Ask an adult to microwave it until warmed through, about 30 seconds. Remove the bowl from the microwave.

Place some of the chicken on a piece of lettuce.

NUTRITION NOTE To make this dish healthier, add shredded carrots or other fresh vegetables to the wrap.

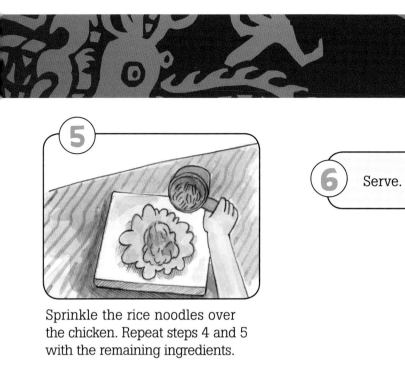

5

Sprinkle the rice noodles over the chicken. Repeat steps 4 and 5 with the remaining ingredients.

6 Serve.

MEAT & BEANS

This Recipe Includes

These sweet, sticky chicken wings are a great snack. They can also be a quick lunch if served with rice or a salad.

Sticky Sesame Wings

INGREDIENTS

1/2 cup hoisin sauce

1 tablespoon rice vinegar

1 teaspoon Chinese
five-spice powder

2 pounds chicken wing
pieces (about 20 wings)

1 tablespoon sesame seeds

TOOLS

large rimmed baking sheet

aluminum foil

cooking spray

large mixing bowl

whisk

clear measuring cup

measuring spoons

wooden spoons

oven mitts

platter

Preheat oven to 475°. Line a large rimmed baking sheet with foil. Spray the foil with cooking spray.

In a large mixing bowl, whisk the hoisin sauce with the rice vinegar and five-spice powder.

Add the wings, and toss them with the sauce until coated.

Transfer the wings to the prepared baking sheet.

16

FOOD FACT★ Hoisin sauce is a popular condiment in China, where it's often used the same way American cooks use barbecue sauce.

5

Ask an adult to bake the wings in the upper third of the oven until browned and cooked through, about 25 minutes, turning them over halfway through.

6

Sprinkle the wings with the sesame seeds.

7 Serve.

17

This Recipe Includes

MEAT & BEANS, VEGETABLES, GRAINS

Fried rice is a popular dish in China, and a popular way to use up day-old rice and other leftover ingredients. Fried rice is usually made in a wok, but this healthier version is baked in the oven.

Not-Fried Rice

INGREDIENTS

1 tablespoon peanut oil
2 large eggs
1 scallion
1/4 cup soy sauce
1 tablespoon Asian
    sesame oil
1 teaspoon garlic powder
2 teaspoons powdered
    ginger
4 cups cooled cooked rice
one 10-ounce bag frozen
    peas and carrots, thawed
1 cup cooked diced ham

TOOLS

8-by-8-inch baking dish
measuring spoons
pastry brush
small mixing bowls
forks
kitchen shears
clear measuring cup
measuring cups
wooden spoon
large mixing bowl
aluminum foil
oven mitts
serving bowl

18

Preheat oven to 375°. Brush the bottom and sides of a baking dish with the peanut oil.

In a small mixing bowl, beat the eggs with a fork.

Using a kitchen shears, cut the scallion greens crosswise into pieces.

In another small mixing bowl, stir the soy sauce with the sesame oil, garlic powder, and powdered ginger.

FUN WITH FOOD★ The next time you have leftover rice, make up your own recipe for fried rice by adding other leftover meat and vegetables.

In a large mixing bowl, combine the cooled cooked rice with the peas, carrots, and ham. Add the soy sauce mixture, and stir until combined.

Add the eggs and scallion greens, and stir again.

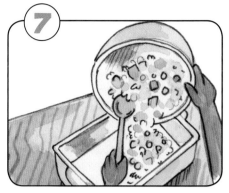

Pour the rice mixture into the prepared baking dish. Ask an adult to cover the dish with aluminum foil and bake it for 20 minutes.

8 Remove the dish from the oven, and stir it with a clean fork. Serve the rice in a serving bowl.

This Recipe Includes

MEAT & BEANS, GRAINS

In China, these dumplings are a popular dish served with *dim sum*, a morning meal consisting of many small dishes.

Dim Sum Dumplings

INGREDIENTS
8 ounces ground pork
1 tablespoon hoisin sauce
1 teaspoon freshly
    grated ginger
1 garlic clove, passed
    through a garlic press
1 tablespoon soy sauce
16 round dumpling
    wrappers (also
    called gyoza)
water, for brushing
    and steaming
dumpling sauce, for serving

TOOLS
large mixing bowl
measuring spoons
garlic press
wooden spoon
small serving bowl
pastry brush
large pot
metal steaming basket
cooking spray
spoon
oven mitts
platter

1 In a large mixing bowl, stir the pork with the hoisin sauce, ginger, garlic, and soy sauce, until combined.

2 Place 8 dumpling wrappers on a clean surface, and brush the edges with water.

3 Place 1 tablespoon of filling in the center of each wrapper.

4 Gather the edges of the wrapper together over the filling, and press them closed. Repeat steps 2 through 4 with the remaining wrappers and filling.

FOOD FACT★ *Dim sum* means "to your heart's content." During dim sum service, small plates of food are served directly off of carts wheeled through the dining room.

5

Fill the pot with ½ inch of water. Place a metal steaming basket in the pot. Spray the steaming basket with cooking spray.

6

Ask an adult to help you with this step: Bring the water to a simmer. Place the dumplings in the steaming basket so they aren't touching (you may have to cook them in batches).

7

Cover the pot, and steam the dumplings until they are cooked through, about 8 minutes.

8 Transfer the dumplings to a platter, and serve with the dumpling sauce.

This Recipe Includes

MEAT & BEANS, VEGETABLES

Soups are an important part of Chinese cuisine. The Chinese believe certain soups have healing powers, much like how many Americans think chicken noodle soup helps cure a cold.

Egg Drop Soup

INGREDIENTS
10 large spinach leaves
2 scallions
2 large eggs
5 cups chicken stock or
    low-sodium broth
1 teaspoon soy sauce
pinch of ground
    white pepper

TOOLS
kitchen shears
measuring cups
fork
clear measuring cup
measuring spoons
large pot
wooden spoon
oven mitts
strainer
ladle
soup bowls

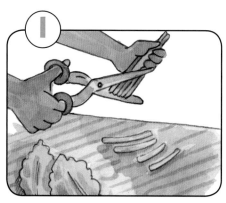

1 Roll the spinach leaves tightly. With a kitchen shears, cut the spinach rolls crosswise, so each cut opens into thin ribbons.

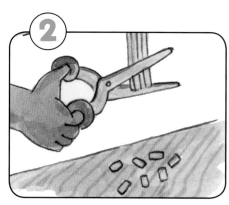

2 With the kitchen shears, cut the scallion greens crosswise into pieces.

3 In a measuring cup, lightly beat the eggs with a fork.

4 Ask an adult to bring the chicken stock, soy sauce, and pepper to a boil in a large pot.

FOOD FACT★ When the eggs touch the hot broth, they turn from a liquid into a solid. This is called coagulation.

5 Remove the pot from the heat. Pour the beaten eggs through a strainer into the broth to make thin ribbons.

6 Add the spinach and scallion greens to the broth.

7 Ladle the soup into bowls, and serve.

This Recipe Includes

MEAT & BEANS

In China, pork is more popular than beef. These sweet-and-sticky ribs are great as a snack, or you can serve them with rice and vegetables for a full meal.

Honey-Hoisin Barbecued Ribs

INGREDIENTS

one 1-inch piece of peeled
    fresh ginger, cut into
    small chunks
2 garlic cloves
2 tablespoons soy sauce
1 tablespoon vegetable oil
1/4 cup hoisin sauce
1 tablespoon honey
1 rack baby back pork ribs
rice, for serving

TOOLS

large rimmed baking sheet
aluminum foil
measuring spoons
clear measuring cup
blender
small serving bowl
pastry brush
oven mitts
metal tongs
serrated knife
platter

Preheat the oven to 400°.

Line a large rimmed baking sheet with foil.

Place the ginger, garlic, soy sauce, vegetable oil, hoisin sauce, and honey in a blender. Blend the mixture until smooth. Set aside half of the sauce in a serving bowl.

Place the ribs, meaty side up, on the prepared baking sheet. Brush them all over with half of the remaining sauce.

FOOD FACT★ The easiest way to peel fresh ginger is with a teaspoon: Hold the ginger in one hand, and use the edge of the spoon to scrape off the peel.

5

Turn the ribs meaty side down. Ask an adult to bake them for 20 minutes.

6

Ask an adult to turn the ribs over and brush them with more sauce. Continue baking them until tender, about 30 minutes longer.

7

When cool enough to handle, ask an adult to cut the rack into individual ribs with a serrated knife.

8 Serve with the rice and the remaining sauce.

MEAT & BEANS, GRAINS

Although they are the most famous dessert in American Chinese restaurants, fortune cookies aren't Chinese at all! They were invented in California about 100 years ago, and quickly became a popular end to Chinese meals.

Fortune Cookies

INGREDIENTS
confectioners' sugar
one 9-inch store-bought pie
    crust, chilled
2 egg whites, lightly beaten

TOOLS
large rimmed baking sheet
cooking spray
nontoxic marker or pen
20 slips of paper, about
    2 inches by 1/2 inch
strainer
3-inch-round cookie cutter
    or drinking glass
rolling pin
small serving bowl
pastry brush
oven mitts

1 Preheat the oven to 375°. Spray a large rimmed baking sheet with cooking spray.

2 With a nontoxic marker or pen, write fortunes on the slips of paper.

3 Using a strainer, dust a clean work surface with confectioners' sugar. Place the pie crust on top of the sugar.

4 Use a round cookie cutter or drinking glass to punch out 3-inch circles of dough. Combine the leftover dough scraps, and roll out the dough. Repeat this step until the dough is gone.

FUN WITH FOOD★ In addition to fortunes, you can write jokes, secret messages, or lucky numbers on the slips of paper.

5

Dust the dough circles with confectioners' sugar.

6

Fold a circle of dough in half over the tips of your index fingers. Then gently fold the ends together to form the shape of a fortune cookie, leaving space for the fortunes. Repeat with the remaining circles.

7

Place the cookies on the prepared baking sheet, about 1 inch apart. Brush the tops of the cookies with the egg whites.

8

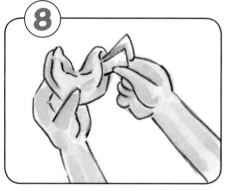

Ask an adult to bake the cookies for 15 minutes, until lightly browned. Let the cookies cool on the pan. Slip the fortunes (you may need to fold the paper) into the cookies.

9 Serve.

VEGETABLES, GRAINS,
MEAT & BEANS

Egg rolls are very popular in China, where people also eat sweet versions for dessert. Egg rolls are usually fried in oil, but these are baked in the oven.

Wrap-n-Bake Egg Rolls

INGREDIENTS
3 scallions
one 16-ounce bag
    coleslaw mix
1 cup chopped
    cooked shrimp
1 tablespoon grated
    fresh ginger
2 tablespoons soy sauce
one 16-ounce package egg
    roll wrappers
water, for dabbing
1 cup sweet and sour sauce,
    for serving

TOOLS
large rimmed baking sheet
cooking spray
kitchen shears
large mixing bowl
measuring cups
measuring spoons
wooden spoons
oven mitts
clear measuring cup
small serving bowl
platter

28

Preheat the oven to 425°.

Spray a large rimmed baking sheet with cooking spray.

With a kitchen shears, cut the scallion greens crosswise into small pieces.

In a large mixing bowl, use wooden spoons to toss the coleslaw mix with the scallion greens, shrimp, ginger, and soy sauce.

FUN WITH FOOD★ Add cooked pork or chicken, instead of shrimp, to the egg rolls.

Place an egg roll wrapper in front of you so it looks like a diamond. Using your finger, dab the top corner with water. Place about ¼ cup of the filling in the center of the wrapper.

Fold the bottom corner of the wrapper over the filling. Fold in the two sides. Roll the filling tightly over the top corner.

Place the egg roll, seam side down, on the baking sheet. Repeat steps 5 and 6 with the remaining ingredients. Lightly coat the tops of the egg rolls with cooking spray.

Ask an adult to bake the egg rolls for 25 minutes, or until golden brown, turning them over halfway through.

9 Serve with the sweet and sour sauce.

The rice grains that coat these meatballs stick out like spikes when you steam them.

Spiky Meatballs

INGREDIENTS

1 1/2 cups uncooked
    rice, rinsed
1 teaspoon salt
2 cups water
2 scallions
one 8-ounce can sliced
    water chestnuts, drained
1 pound ground chicken
1 cup grated carrot
2 tablespoons soy sauce
2 teaspoons Asian sesame oil
1 teaspoon sugar
1 tablespoon cornstarch
water for steaming
lettuce leaves

TOOLS

measuring cups
medium-sized mixing bowl
measuring spoons
clear measuring cup
strainer
spoon
platters
kitchen shears
table knife
cutting board
large mixing bowl
wooden spoon
large saucepan
metal steaming basket
oven mitts

30

Place the rinsed rice in a medium-sized mixing bowl, and add the salt. Cover the rice with water, and let it soak for 2 hours. Strain the rice, and spread it on a platter.

With a kitchen shears, cut the scallions crosswise into small pieces.

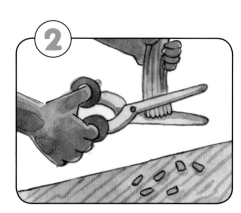

Ask an adult to use a table knife to chop the water chestnuts into very small pieces.

Place the ground chicken, carrot, scallion greens, and water chestnuts in a large mixing bowl, and stir with a wooden spoon to combine. Add the soy sauce, sesame oil, sugar, and cornstarch. Stir until well mixed.

5 Using wet hands, form the chicken mixture into 1-inch balls, and place them on a platter (you should have enough for about 24 balls).

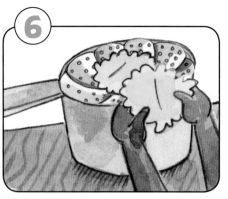

6 Fill a large saucepan with about ½ inch of water. Place a metal steaming basket in the saucepan. Line it with the lettuce leaves.

7 Roll the meatballs in the rice until coated.

8 Arrange half of the meatballs on the lettuce leaves, leaving space between each ball.

9 Ask an adult to steam the meatballs over boiling water for 10 minutes, until the chicken is cooked through and the rice is soft. Repeat with the remaining balls.

10 Serve.

INDEX

INTERNET SITES

FactHound offers a safe, fun way to find Internet sites related to this book. All of the sites have been researched by our staff.

Here's all you do:

Visit *www.facthound.com*

FactHound will fetch the best sites for you!

KIDS DISH